Homemade vegan cheese, yoghurt and milk

Homemade vegan cheese yoghurt and milk

Yvonne Hölzl-Singh

GRUB STREET • LONDON

Published in 2018 by

Grub Street

4 Rainham Close

London

SW11 6SS

Email: food@grubstreet.co.uk

Web: www.grubstreet.co.uk

Twitter: @grub_street

Facebook: Grub Street Publishing

Book and cover design: Daniele Roa

Photography: All photos are by the author

The photo of the author on page 140 is by Arnold Poschl

Copyright © 2017 Eugen Ulmer KG, Stuttgart, Germany

Originally published in German as *Vegan & Selbst Gemacht, Käse, Joghurt, Tofu, Milch*

A CIP catalogue record for this book is available from the British Library.

ISBN 978-1-911621-00-3

Printed and bound by Finidr, Czech Republic

Dear readers,

About four years ago, I began to look into vegan nutrition. My first thought was, "I could never give up cheese." And it was difficult to image a caffé latte without milk. Whenever I visited a vegan friend for coffee, I would always take some cow's milk with me.

Yet, I do not think it is a coincidence if a thought keeps pursuing me. So three and a half years ago, I embarked on a little test: a two-week "milk-free challenge". This short period seemed to me to be quite radical at the time. The two weeks passed by really well. I extended them and, since then, I have been following a vegan diet.

Vegan nutrition should not be seen as a deprivation. It opens up a colourful new world where you can discover lots of new foodstuffs and flavours. The savoury flavour described as 'umami' is however not present in vegan food. Nevertheless, it does make an appearance on the vegan menu where fermented cheese is concerned.

A friend of mine was delighted when she tried my vegan cheese for the first time. Beaming, she said, "Wow, how I have missed this taste!" Although I have been experimenting intensively with vegan cheese over the past year, I am always delighted with every new successful recipe as I missed the taste in my diet a great deal.

However, in this book, I want to introduce you to more than just vegan cheese recipes. The book is also intended to be a reference work when making vegan milk products, cream, yoghurt and tofu, etc. at home.

Have fun trying out my recipes and enjoying vegan food!

Yvonne Hölzl-Singh

Contents

Essentials

Here you will find all the information
you need about the basic essentials,
ingredients and machines needed
to make vegan cheese, tofu, cream,
yoghurt and drinks.

Brief overview

This book is aimed at all those wishing to follow a vegan diet, anyone with a lactose intolerance, and those who are simply interested in trying out something new. It is intended to be a guide about the options for replacing milk products with vegan ones and reinterpreting them.

I start off with cheese and tofu. Then you will find recipes for all kinds of vegan cream and preparing yoghurt. In the third part, I introduce various vegan options for replacing cows' milk. Finally, there are a few piquant and sweet recipes made with vegan cheese, mascarpone and quark alternatives.

I have quite consciously not attempted to imitate special cows' milk cheese varieties. Rather, the recipes should be understood to be vegan nut-cheese creations. In contrast to commercially produced vegan cheeses, yoghurts and milk products, the results with your homemade versions will always turn out a little differently. The production conditions are never exactly the same and little differences such as the brand of soya milk used or the yoghurt starter, the room temperature and humidity, the length of time spent soaking the nuts and seeds and the fermentation period can have an influence on your yoghurt and cheese.

I always state the minimum time for storing a homemade product but this should not be seen as the expiry date. Vegan cheeses, creams and yoghurts often keep for longer depending on the temperature and storage conditions.

As to how heavy a cheese will be depends on the length of time the nuts and seeds have soaked for. In the case of tofu, it depends on the quantity of soya beans used in the soya milk. This is why you will find only a rough weight estimate in the quantities given in the recipes.

Note

The description 'cheese' (and yoghurt, quark, etc.) for products that are not produced from animal milk contravenes the EU's food labelling regulations. As this regulation however only applies to products put on the market, the guideline does not affect the recipes published in this book which are not put on the market. As a result, the author and the publisher have decided to use the term 'cheese' for ease of comprehension (and without inverted commas for readability).

Fermentation starter

The fermentation starter is the basis for vegan cheese production. This can be rejuvelac, kombucha, sauerkraut juice or a yoghurt starter.

Rejuvelac

Rejuvelac is a fermented drink made from grains or pseudograins. First, you germinate seeds such as spelt, wheat or rye, millet or quinoa and then leave them in water until a milky liquid forms that smells slightly cheesy. All the cheeses in this book are made with spelt rejuvelac but you can experiment with other types of grain. Rejuvelac also tastes different with every grain or pseudograin variety used.

Kombucha

Kombucha is also a fermented drink that develops with the help of the kombucha culture (scoby) from tea and sugar. In the case of a kombucha culture, it is not a single culture but a symbiosis of bacteria and yeast. You will find recipes to create both fermentation starters in the book (rejuvelac p. 22, kombucha p. 24).

Sauerkraut juice and yoghurt starters

Cheese can also be fermented with sauerkraut juice or a yoghurt starter. Rejuvelac produces the 'cheesiest' taste, however. When buying a yoghurt starter, make sure that it is a vegan one.

Kombucha

Ingredients used

In most cases, nuts, seeds and soya beans are the basis for vegan alternatives to cheese and milk. They can be used to make vegan cheese, vegan drinks, vegan milk products and vegan yoghurt.

Nuts, seeds and soya beans

Nuts, seeds and soya beans are primarily used as base products for producing vegan cheese. The most common vegan cheeses in this book are based on cashew nuts or almonds. Macadamia nuts can also be used to make cheese. For reasons of economy, I have only used them in this book in the recipe for grated cheese. As cashew nuts are not entirely cheap, it is worth buying them in large quantities when they are on offer.

Soya

Soya is a product that can cause allergies in some people. Therefore, in the case of cheese, I have used soya only in a cream cheese recipe. There are also a few recipes based on

Nuts are the base ingredient for vegan cheeses

soya in the Cream, Yoghurt & Co section. Working with soya yoghurt is less laborious, but it is not always the fastest method for making some alternative milk products such as crème fraîche or sour cream. In my opinion, the soya-free alternatives taste better, however. Apart from quark, there are also soya-free versions of all the recipes in the book. This applies to the yoghurt recipes, too.

Coagulants and emulsifying agents

Nigari are small white crystals used to coagulate soya milk in traditional Japanese tofu production. It is easiest to obtain nigari on line.

Sunflower lecithin is required to make vegan butter so that the solid fat combines with the water phase and the mixture emulsifies.

Thickening agents

Coconut cooking fat, agar agar, starches, xanthan, carageen, tapioca flour and arrowroot are used in vegan cheeses as thickening agents and stabilisers.

Coconut cooking fat, agar agar and cornflour have been used for the recipes in this book. But beware – do not confuse coconut cooking fat with coconut oil. It is a taste-less, refined, deodorised coconut oil. Coconut oil, on the

Good to Know—

Nigari is an agent originally acquired from sea water and can be purchased both in the traditionally produced form and artificially made. Some suppliers decided only to sell nigari produced in a laboratory following the nuclear catastrophe in Fukushima.

other hand, has a strong taste that would interfere with the production of vegan cheese. In the case of coconut cooking fat or refined coconut oil, the taste substances are removed from the oil by steam deodorisation.

Flavouring agents

Yeast flakes are often used in vegan cheese as a flavouring agent. But light types of miso, garlic and onions – fresh or even granules or powder – mustard, tomato purée, lemon juice, umeboshi plums and fresh or dried herbs are also used in vegan cheese production. Miso, lemon juice and mustard should be added in very careful doses so that they do not overpower the taste of the cheese.

Dried herb mixtures are suitable for sprinkling or coating the cheese , such as *herbes de Provence*. Also paprika, or depending on the variety of cheese, fresh, chopped herbs, tomato granules or red pepper.

Possible flavouring agents for vegan cheese

Useful equipment

For the majority of the recipes in this book, a stick blender is sufficient. You do not necessarily need an expensive high-powered blender. Soya milk machines and yoghurt makers are useful, but not absolutely necessary.

High-powered blender

As every household does not have a high-powered blender, I have made all the cheese varieties with a stick blender. However, for various drinks, raw vegan yoghurts and vegan cheese fondue, you will need a high-powered blender, or at least a very powerful one as the smaller blender will not be able to chop the nuts finely enough.

In principle, a high-powered blender is recommended for vegan cookery in general. When making smaller portions of cheese, it is occasionally easier to work with a smaller blender as you can remove the smaller quantity of cheese mixture more easily than from the bowl of a large blender.

Soya milk machine

If you wish to make soya milk on a regular basis, I recommend investing in a soya milk machine. It facilitates the process considerably. The machine boils the beans, chops and filters them. You can use the milk immediately, or filter it through a nut milk bag once again to remove the fine pieces of soya bean.

It is, of course, possible to make soya drinks in a saucepan; it is just more laborious. To make soya milk in a saucepan, you will need a high-powered mixer. Soya milk machines usually have their own in-built programmes for making nut drinks, which can be interesting for households without a high-powered mixer.

Jars and moulds for making cheese, tofu and yoghurt

Yoghurt makers

For the soya yoghurt recipes you will need a yoghurt maker, as it heats up the yoghurt during the fermentation process. You do not need a yoghurt maker for the nut yoghurt recipes. A warm place in your home is sufficient.

Nut milk bag

When I first started making almond milk on a daily basis, I found a nut milk bag to be superfluous, as the liquid can be sieved through a muslin. At some point, I introduced a nut milk bag into the kitchen, and now I could not do without it. It is quicker and easier to use and clean. As alternatives you can use a straining cloth, a fine cotton cloth or muslin, tea-towel or new cloth nappy.

Cheese moulds

It is not absolutely necessary to buy cheese moulds either, although it is fun to work with the right one. You can use small kitchen tins, muffin tins, little bowls, small gratin dishes, storage boxes, or, for firmer cheeses, cooking rings shaped as circles, hearts or squares. You can fill muffin and small silicon baking moulds with the cheese immediately.

Good to Know —

If you use rigid moulds, you should line them with cling film. This also applies to bought cheese moulds as these are actually made for cheese which has to drain, which is why they have holes.

Other useful equipment

A tofu press is useful for preparing tofu. You will need greaseproof paper and cling film to make cheese.
And small glasses for the yoghurt maker. To strain various vegan milk products based on soya yoghurt, you will need a large sieve, a cotton cloth and a bowl or pot that is deeper than the sieve.

To ferment grains for rejuvelac and other vegan milk products at room temperature, half-litre preserving jars are very useful covered with a cotton cloth or paper towel. You will need robust rubber bands to fix the cloth in place.

One-litre glass bottles or large jars with screw-top lids are suitable for vegan drinks. For homemade drinks, I like to use half-litre preserving jars with screw-top lids. These can be washed easily in the dishwasher whereas bottles are more laborious to clean.

Vegan drinks are very easy to make yourself

And off we go...

From now on, you can make all your own vegan milk products from cheese to yoghurt yourself quite simply. Homemade simply tastes the best!

Cheese

On the raw food scene, vegan cheese is produced using nuts and seeds with various fermentation starters. This is what the recipes in this book are based on. It is true that there are various versions of vegan cheese offered in shops, but speaking as a former cheese lover, the cheesy taste is often missing. But with a little effort and patience, you can create it yourself through the fermentation process.

Making your own vegan cheese is not a lot of work but because there are long waiting times between the individual stages in cheese production, it does require time. There is little difference in this respect between making vegan nut cheeses and dairy cheese.

But the waiting times are necessary to allow the taste to develop. Once you have made vegan cheese yourself you will never want to miss out on the taste again.

What are the advantages of the different types of fermentation?

The vegan cheese with the strongest cheese taste is one fermented with rejuvelac. From my point of view, this is the top choice. Kombucha goes well with the slightly sweetish Gervais. In my view, sauerkraut juice and yoghurt starters are the beginners' versions for all those who are a bit nervous at the start of making their own rejuvelac. If you miss the taste of dairy cheese, look out for the recipes using rejuvelac. The taste will be worth the extra work!

The fermentation time can vary depending on the temperature and humidity. There are no hard and fast rules about how long the process takes. Keep a close eye on the cheese during the fermentation process and taste it to see if it has reached the desired level of ripeness. The longer it ferments, the stronger it will taste. In summer it will be quicker than in winter. The fermentation time in the recipes should therefore be adapted to the corresponding season and temperature.

Drinks and Cream

Homemade vegan drinks have lots of advantages: they usually taste better than commercially produced drinks, you know what is in them, you save money and create less waste. Soya, rice and millet drinks have to be cooked. All the others in the book are raw.

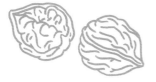

To make many of these drinks, you will need a powerful mixer, but there are also recipes for which a less powerful one is sufficient. It is simply a matter of taste as to whether you want to just sieve the liquid, or filter it through a nut

Homemade vegan drinks taste better

milk bag or cotton cloth. Personally, I like my drinks well filtered, and I even filter the soya milk again once it has come out of the soya milk machine.

In addition to soya beans, basic ingredients for vegan milk alternatives are nuts, cashews and seeds, such as sesame and hempseed. Grains and pseudograins like oats, buckwheat and millet are also suitable for making milk alternatives.

Various techniques are used for vegan cream recipes. The alternatives to milk products are fermented with rejuvelac, and well drained soya yoghurt works well as a base for crème fraîche and quark. Cashew nuts and coconut milk are used as a base for various vegan cream alternatives. There are also soya-free versions for almost all the vegan milk products in this book.

Yoghurt

Yoghurt has a life of its own, and even little changes to the recipe such as using a different brand of soya milk or starter can make it thinner or thicker. Nor is the composition of homemade soya milk always exactly the same. The exact content of soya depends on how much liquid evaporates during the production process. For this reason, it requires tenacity and patience if you want to make the perfect vegan yoghurt. I recommend that you always use the same brand of soya milk and starter and to use this combination to simply adapt the yoghurt to your own needs.

My experience shows that the raw cashew and almond yoghurt versions are easier to make. If they turn out to be too thick, they can easily be thinned down to the right consistency with a little water. They will become firmer once chilled and will become slightly acidic in the refrigerator. They should be stirred before using.

Tofu

In the case of tofu, the soya milk is coagulated by acidification so that the whey separates from the solid protein components. These are caught by a tofu press and made into a firm block.

Good to Know —

When making yoghurt, it is particularly important that the utensils used are clean to avoid unwanted micro-organisms multiplying. The starter liquid should only be lukewarm as the yoghurt starter cannot tolerate high temperatures.

In China, they traditionally used gypsum (calcium sulphate) for the coagulation process, whereas in Japan nagari flakes (magnesium chloride) derived from sea water are used.. However, you can also start the coagulation of the soya milk with lemon juice or vinegar. Its consistency will be somewhat crumbly and coarser. You will find recipes for both versions in this book.

If you do not like the taste of soya or cannot tolerate it, you will find a Burmese version of tofu which is made out of gram (chickpea) flour. Known as shan tofu, it can be eaten raw, as a salad, deep-fried or baked. It can also be used to replace mozzarella and is delicious deep-fried with a little soy sauce and sesame oil, and also lukewarm on salad (p.82)

Rejuvelac

Rejuvelac can be made from various grains or pseudograin types. It forms the basis of many cheese recipes in this book.

Ingredients

100 g spelt grains *or* wheat, rye, millet, for example

750 g filtered water *or* still mineral water

Servings

Makes about 750 ml

- Soak the spelt grains in water overnight, ensuring they are completely covered.

- The next morning, rinse and drain the grains, and return to the jar and cover with fabric or kitchen towel with a rubber band. Rinse the grains once or twice a day depending on the room temperature, so that they are always damp but are not standing in water.

- Put the jars in a warm place but not in direct sunlight until the first sprouts appear. This will take between half a day and two days depending on the temperature and type of grain.

- As soon as the first little tails are visible on the grains, rinse them through again and put in a one-litre jar and pour the filtered water on top. When starting rejuvelac, do not use tap water because it contains chlorine and will spoil the rejuvelac.

- Cover the jars with a cloth and fasten with a rubber band. Leave the rejuvelac for one to three days – depending on room temperature – until the liquid is milky and acidic and smells like cheese.

- Strain off the rejuvelac, decant into bottles and store in the refrigerator.

- The rejuvelac can be kept in the refrigerator for about five days. If necessary, the rejuvelac can be frozen, but it ferments the cheese more effectively when it is fresh.

Tip — The quickest way to rinse the grains is to add water to the jar, then put a small sieve over the mouth of the jar, tip the jar upside down and drain the water from the jar.

Kombucha

The Kombucha culture is not a single culture, it is made up of a symbiosis of cultures and bacteria. Kombucha also forms the base for some cheese recipes in this book. It can however also be enjoyed as a healthy drink.

Ingredients

2 litres water
150-200 g raw cane sugar
15 g black *and/or* green tea
1 Kombucha culture (scoby)
20 ml starter liquid

Also:
A 2.5-3 litre capacity jar *or* porcelain container with a wide neck
A cotton cloth for covering the jar
A rubber band

Servings

Makes about 2 litres

• Bring the water to the boil in a large saucepan and add the sugar and tea. Allow the tea to infuse for 15 minutes and then cool down to room temperature. The tea must be completely cooled or only just slightly lukewarm so that the 'culture' does not die. The kombucha culture prefers a blend of black and green tea. But it will also work if you mix in other teas. Flavoured teas can be used from time to time, but not constantly. This would damage the culture.

• Rinse the container well to remove any possible residue of washing-up liquid. The culture cannot tolerate this. Put the kombucha mushroom with its smooth side facing up into the container with the starter liquid. Add the cooled tea. Leave space at the top of the container as the scoby needs air. Cover the container with a cotton cloth and fasten with the rubber band. Put the kombucha in a warm place and leave it to ferment. Direct sunlight will damage the culture.

• The drink will be ready after 7–16 days. If the kombucha infuses for only a short period, it may contain residual alcohol from the fermentation process. The fermentation time depends on the room temperature and also on

Continues overleaf ⟶

the thickness of the culture. The longer the kombucha ferments, the more acidic it will become.

• Strain the kombucha through a cotton cloth. Reserve 20 ml of the starter liquid, pour the remainder into bottles and store in the refrigerator.

• Every time you make a new batch, clean the culture thoroughly with lukewarm water and remove all the yeast strings. Also wash the starter jar for new batches without using washing-up liquid. Proceed in the same way for the next round. Put the culture with the starter liquid and the sweetened and cooled tea in the container, close and let it ferment in a warm place.

• Over time, the kombucha culture will become quite thick. Divide the culture and either dispose of the lower part or use it to cultivate a new batch of kombucha. There are instructions about how to do this on the internet. Sometimes the culture sinks down in the jar and a new culture forms on the surface. In this event, the sunken culture can be disposed of.

• The kombucha can be kept in the refrigerator for about four to six weeks. Finished batches can often be kept considerably longer. It will turn slightly acidic in the refrigerator.

Tip — You can purchase a culture from an on-line shop, or obtain one as a gift from friends.

Tip — I like kombucha best in summer after it has fermented for a week with 200 g raw cane sugar. Most kombucha aficionados leave it to ferment for longer. If sometimes it is a bit acidic I like to use it for making cheese.

Cheese and tofu

In this chapter, I reveal my very favourite vegan cheese and tofu recipes. They range from quick cream cheeses to laboriously matured cheese varieties to truffle and cheese pralines for your next party.

Basic cashew cheese

This recipe can be used for cashew cream cheese.
You can make the basic recipe into a herby cream cheese roll,
a creamy cashew cheese or an olive and cashew cheese.
This is my favourite cream cheese.

Ingredients

150 g cashew nuts

30 ml rejuvelac

¼ tsp Himalayan salt

Servings

Makes about 235 g

• Soak the cashew nuts in water for about eight hours or overnight.

• Then drain, rinse in water and purée with the other ingredients in a blender to make a smooth mixture. The quantity of rejuvelac depends on the exact soaking time and the mixer. Use only as much liquid as necessary to produce a smooth mixture.

• Put the cheese in a glass or ceramic bowl and cover with a plate. Allow the cashew cheese to ripen for half a day to two days depending on the temperature. Taste from time to time to see if it has developed the required taste.

• Put the cheese in the refrigerator and chill for a few hours or continue to ripen as required.

• This cashew cheese will keep in the refrigerator for about a week.

Tip — Depending on how strong you want the cheese to taste, leave it to ripen for 12-48 hours. The taste will be stronger the longer you leave it. Room temperature influences the length of time it takes to ripen.

Tip — You can quickly create more cheese varieties using 1-2 tbsp green or red pesto, depending on your mood.

Basic almond cheese

Almond cheese can be used as a version of vegan cream cheese. It can be made into walnut and almond cheese, tomato and rosemary cheese, almond and paprika cheese, and baked almond cheese, or truffle and cheese pralines.

Ingredients

150 g almonds, blanched

60–70 ml rejuvelac or kombucha

½ tsp Himalayan salt

Servings

Makes about 280 g

- Soak the almonds in water for at least twenty-four hours.

- Rinse the almonds and mix with the rejuvelac or kombucha and the salt in a blender until smooth. Stop the blender from time to time, scrape the mixture down to the blade and start again. The quantity of liquid required depends on the blender and the precise amount of time spent soaking the almonds. Use only as much liquid as the mixer needs to produce a homogenous mass.

- Put the cheese in a glass or ceramic bowl and cover with a plate.

- Allow to ripen at room temperature for 24–48 hours depending on how strong you want it to taste. Taste from time to time to see if the cheese has developed the required taste. It will ripen faster in warmer temperatures than in cooler rooms where it takes a little longer.

- To halt the ripening process, put the cheese in the refrigerator or continue to ripen as required.

- This cheese will keep in the refrigerator for about a week.

Tip — You can blanch the almonds simply by pouring boiling water over them and leaving them for a few minutes in the water. Then check to see if the skins come away easily. If so, drain and peel. This saves money and is really quick.

Cream cheese
with sauerkraut juice

This recipe can also be seen as a basic recipe.
You can decorate the cheese with herbs, onion or garlic
granules, dried tomatoes, yeast flakes or spices, as you wish.
Or enjoy it as a fine cream cheese.

Ingredients

150 g almonds, blanched
70 ml sauerkraut juice
½ tsp Himalayan salt

Servings

Makes about 280 g

- Soak the almonds in water for 24 hours, drain, rinse and together with the sauerkraut juice and salt, process in a blender until a creamy mixture forms. Mix in several batches and scrape the mixture down to the blade from time to time.

- Put the cheese mixture in a ceramic or glass bowl, cover with a plate and leave to ripen for one or two days. Taste from time to time to see if the cheese has developed the required taste. It will ripen faster in warmer temperatures than in cooler rooms where it take a little longer.

- Then shape the cheese into a loaf or press it into a container lined with cling film. If the mixture is too soft, it can be chilled before putting it in the container. Chill for a couple of hours in the refrigerator before serving.

- The cheese can be kept in the refrigerator for about five days.

Cashew cheese
with yoghurt starter

*Vegan nut cheese can also be made with a yoghurt starter.
For the sake of completeness, I would also like to include
this version. But cheese fermented with rejuvelac tastes
considerably 'cheesier'.*

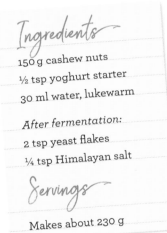

Ingredients

150 g cashew nuts
½ tsp yoghurt starter
30 ml water, lukewarm

After fermentation:
2 tsp yeast flakes
¼ tsp Himalayan salt

Servings

Makes about 230 g

• Soak the almonds in water for 24 hours, drain, rinse and together with the sauerkraut juice and salt, process in a blender until a creamy mixture forms. Mix in several batches and scrape the mixture down to the blade from time to time.

• Put the cheese mixture in a ceramic or glass bowl, cover with a plate and leave to ripen for one or two days. Taste from time to time to see if the cheese has developed the required taste. It will ripen faster in warmer temperatures than in cooler rooms where it takes a little longer.

• Then shape the cheese into a loaf or press it into a container lined with cling film. If the mixture is too soft, it can be chilled before putting it in the container. Chill for a couple of hours in the refrigerator before serving.

• The cheese can be kept in the refrigerator for about five days.

Herby cream cheese roll

These easy herby cream cheese rolls can be made with seasonal herbs, as desired.

Ingredients

1½ cloves garlic

2–3 tbsp chopped mixed herbs, (e.g. rosemary, wild garlic, lemon balm, oregano, chives, parsley)

1 portion of basic cashew cheese (see p. 30), ripened for 1-2 days

2 tsp yeast flakes, slightly heaped

½ tsp Himalayan salt

4 tbsp chopped chives, for sprinkling

Servings

Makes two small cream cheese rolls

- Peel the garlic clove and crush with a garlic press.

- Wash and dry the herbs and chop finely.

- Apart from the chives, mix all the ingredients together well, put the mixture in a thick strand on greaseproof paper. Roll up into a sausage shape, twist the ends together and chill in the refrigerator for a few hours.

- Then undo the roll carefully. Divide into two small rolls and roll in chopped chives before serving.

Tip — Vary the herbs according to the season and your preferences. I particularly love eating this cheese with a few lavender flowers, or in spring with freshly picked wild garlic.

Horseradish gervais

I always loved horseradish gervais before I became a vegan which is why I had to include it in this book.

Ingredients

150 g cashew nuts

¼ tsp sea salt

30 ml kombucha

2–5 tsp horseradish, grated

¼ tsp Himalayan salt

Servings

Makes about 250 g

- Soak the cashew nuts in water for four to eight hours.

- Rinse the cashew nuts and mix with the kombucha and sea salt in a blender until smooth. If necessary, stop the blender from time to time to scrape the cheese down towards the blade. Then start mixing again.

- Put the mixture in a glass or ceramic bowl and cover with a plate. Allow the cheese to ripen for one-and-a-half to two days at room temperature, depending on how warm it is.

- Mix the ripened cheese in the blender with the grated horse-radish, and season to taste with salt. If the horseradish is mild, more can be added.

- Chill for a few hours in the refrigerator before serving.

- The cheese can be kept in the refrigerator for about five days.

Soya cream cheese

This simple soya cream cheese can be used as soon as it has drained. You can also make it into a herby version.

Ingredients

500 ml soya yoghurt

Herb version:

3 tbsp chopped mixed herbs

2 tsp capers

1 tsp Dijon mustard

1 tsp yeast extract paste

¼ tsp Himalayan salt

Servings

Makes about 270 g, depending on how long it takes to drain

There are two options when making soya cream cheese:

- Place a cotton cloth or a clean cloth nappy in a large sieve which is on top of a small bowl. Fill the cloth with the yoghurt, put the bowl in the refrigerator and let it drain to reach the desired consistency. This will take between one-and-a-half and two days depending on the yoghurt and the desired consistency.

- For the second option, put the cloth in a bowl and add the yoghurt. Tie up the opposite ends of the cloth, hang up the resulting bag and place the bowl under the bag to catch the whey. The bag can be hung on an upper kitchen cupboard. Shops sell devices with fabric bags for draining cream cheese. These can be attached to bowls or sauce-pans. The second option will only work if you have a cool, pest-free place where the yoghurt can drain. The draining process is quicker in this option.

- Chill the drained soya cream cheese in the refrigerator for a few hours to use it solely as cream cheese.

- For the herb version, finely chop the herbs and capers. Mix all the ingredients into the cream cheese, season to taste and chill before enjoying on fresh bread.

Tip — If desired, you can also mix spring onions, onions, or fresh wild garlic in season, into the cream cheese.

Pumpkin seed and cashew cheese

Like nuts, pumpkin seeds are a great source of protein and unsaturated fats, including omega-3. They also contain iron, selenium, calcium, B vitamins and beta-carotene. So this cheese is a powerhouse of nutrients.

Ingredients

100 g pumpkin seeds
100 g cashew nuts
½ tsp Himalayan salt
50-60 ml rejuvelac
1 tbsp pumpkin seed oil

Servings

Makes about 350 g

- Soak the pumpkin seeds and cashew nuts overnight in water.

- The next day pour off the water, rinse and drain.

- Then put the nuts and seeds with the remaining ingredients in a blender and mix until you have a fine, creamy mixture. Stop the blender several times throughout the process and scrape the mixture down towards the blade. The quantity of rejuvelac required depends greatly on the blender used and the time spent soaking. You need to achieve a smooth, soft mixture.

- Put the cheese in a glass or ceramic bowl, cover with a plate and allow to ferment for around twenty-four hours at room temperature. The longer it ferments, the stronger it will taste. In contrast to the other cheeses, do not leave this cheese to ferment for longer than twenty-four hours, particularly in the summer. The oil can cause it to go off!

- The cheese can be kept in the refrigerator for about five days.

Creamy cashew cheese

This creamy cheese can be cut into slices easily when chilled and yet is soft and creamy. It is one of my favourite classics and can be creatively adapted to make different versions.

Ingredients

1 portion of basic cashew
    cheese (see p. 30),
    ripened for 1-2 days
100 g coconut cooking
    fat, liquid *or* very soft
2 tsp yeast flakes
¾ tsp Himalayan salt

Optional:
Dried herbs for sprinkling

Servings

Makes about 325 g

- Put all the ingredients in the blender and mix until smooth and creamy and the salt has dissolved.

- Fill three cups in a muffin tray made of silicon, or little tins lined with cling film, smooth out with the back of a damp dessert spoon and put in the refrigerator until the cheese is firm.

- Remove the cheese from the mould, and sprinkle with seasoning, if desired.

- The cheese can be kept in the refrigerator for about five days.

Tip — This cheese can be used as a baked topping on dishes or on pizza. I also like to eat it with boiled potatoes.

Cashew cheese
with olives

*I particularly love this olive and cashew cheese.
It is a wonderful addition to a vegan cheese board.*

Ingredients

1 portion of basic cashew
   cheese (see p. 30),
   ripened for one-and-
   a-half to two days
100 g coconut cooking
   fat, liquid *or* very soft
1 tsp barley miso *or*
   another light miso
¾ tsp Himalayan salt
40 g pitted green olives
Black olives,
   for decoration

Servings

Makes about 380 g

- Put all the ingredients except the olives in a blender and mix until you have a smooth, homogenous mixture.

- Chop the olives roughly and mix in.

- Line two moulds with cling film, if desired, add the mixture and smooth down with the back of a damp dessert spoon. Put the cheese in the refrigerator for several hours to harden before serving.

- Release the cheese from the mould, decorate with black olives and serve with a freshly baked baguette and a glass of red wine.

- The cheese can be kept in the refrigerator for about five days.

Tip — This cheese can be used as a baked topping on dishes or on pizza.

Walnut and almond cheese

This walnut and almond cheese is one of the strongest-tasting cheeses in this book. It tastes good on pizza and is suitable for gratins.

1 portion of basic almond
   cheese (see p. 32),
   ripened for 1-2 days
80 g coconut cooking fat,
   liquid *or* very soft
1½ tsp yeast flakes
½ tsp Himalayan salt
30 g walnuts

Also:
A few nice walnut halves
   for decorating

Servings
Makes about 385 g

- Put the almond cheese with the coconut cooking fat and yeast flakes in a blender and mix until you have a fine, homogenous mixture. Stop the blender several times throughout the process and scrape the mixture down towards the blade.

- Line a cheese mould with cling film and put a third of the mixture in it. Set another third of the mixture to one side.

- Put the remaining third into the blender with the walnuts and blitz until the nuts are coarsely chopped. Spread the mixture on top of the first third and press down with the back of a spoon. Add the remaining third to the mould, press down firmly and close the cling film over the top of the cheese. Leave the cheese to firm up for several hours in the refrigerator.

- Before serving, remove the cling film from the cheese and decorate with walnuts.

- The cheese can be kept in the refrigerator for about five days.

Tomato and rosemary cheese

This variation on a Mediterreanean cheese with tomatoes and rosemary will also pep up the look of any vegan cheese board.

Ingredients

40 g dried tomatoes in oil
1 portion of basic almond
  cheese (see p. 32),
  ripened for 1-2 days
1 clove of garlic
1½ tbsp chopped
  rosemary
20 g coconut cooking fat,
  liquid *or* soft
1 tbsp tomato purée
Some freshly ground
  pepper
A little Himalayan salt

Servings

Makes about 350 g

- Drain the dried tomatoes and chop.

- Put all the ingredients in a blender and mix until the garlic is chopped up and the tomatoes are reduced to small pieces. Season to taste with salt and freshly ground pepper.

- Place cooking rings on greaseproof paper, pour the cheese into the rings and press down with a spoon.

- Chill the cheese in the refrigerator for several hours and then carefully press the cheese out of the rings.

- The cheese can be kept in the refrigerator for about five days.

Almond and paprika cheese

This almond and paprika cheese is particularly recommended for aficionados of stronger-tasting cheeses.

Ingredients

1 portion of basic almond
cheese (see p. 32),
ripened for 1-2 days
40 g coconut cooking fat,
soft *or* liquid
1 tsp granulated onion
1 tsp granulated garlic
1 tsp paprika, mild
1½ tsp yeast flakes
Paprika for sprinkling

Servings

Makes about 320 g

- Put all the ingredients in a blender and mix until you have a smooth, creamy mixture. Stop the machine several times throughout the process and push the mixture down towards the blade, then continue mixing. Taste the cheese and season if necessary with a little Himalayan salt.

- Place cling film in a small bowl, add the mixture and press down with the back of a damp spoon. Chill in the refrigerator for several hours.

- Dust the cheese with mild paprika before serving. Depending on the shape of the bowl, the cheese can be made into a loaf after chilling.

- The cheese can be kept in the refrigerator for about five days.

Baked almond cheese

*This baked almond cheese can be served warm or cold.
I particularly like it when it is warm on rocket or a colourful
leaf salad. Of course, I love all the cheeses described in this
book, but this is a favourite.*

Ingredients

10 g onions

1 clove of garlic

1 portion of basic almond
cheese (see p. 32),
ripened for 1-2 days

50 g ground almonds,
blanched

20–30 g ground almonds
or pumpkin seeds for
the coating

Servings

Makes 7 portions, each
approx 45 g

- Preheat the oven to 180°C, gas 4.

- In the meantime, coarsely chop the onion and garlic.
Mix all the ingredients – except the ingredients for
the coating – in a blender, until you have a homogenous
mixture.

- Take approximately 45 g of the mixture and form it into
little balls, then flatten.

- Then roll the cheese in the ground pumpkin seeds or
almonds and place on a baking sheet lined with greaseproof paper.

- Bake in the pre-heated oven for approximately ten minutes until light golden brown. This cheese tastes delicious
warm or cold.

- The cheese can be kept in the refrigerator for about
five days.

Truffle cheese pralines

*These truffle cheese pralines will be a talking point
at your vegan buffet party. They are delicious both baked or
not, and served hot or cold. Baking them will give them
a firmer consistency.*

Ingredients

1 portion of basic almond
   cheese (see p. 32),
   ripened for 1-2 days
100 g ground almonds,
   blanched
2 tbsp truffle oil
½ tsp Himalayan salt
1 tsp yeast flakes

For garnishing:
Sesame seeds, black
   sesame seeds, dried
   mixed seasoning,
   sweet paprika powder,
   chopped pumpkin
   seeds, chopped
   walnuts, chopped
   pistachio nuts,
   tomato granules

Servings

Makes 19 balls of
   approx. 20 g each

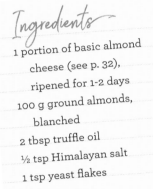

- Put all the ingredients in a blender and mix until you have a fine, creamy mixture.

- Take 20g of the cheese and roll it into a small ball, then roll it in one of the garnishing ingredients, as desired. Repeat until you have used all the cheese.

- Chill in the refrigerator briefly and then serve. Alternatively, bake on greaseproof paper in a pre-heated oven at 180°C, gas 4 for about 10 minutes until light golden brown. They are delicious when baked and can be served hot or cold.

- The cheese can be kept in the refrigerator for about five days.

Tip — These truffle cheese pralines are delicious served hot with salad.

Millet cheese

*This millet cheese is a slightly different vegan variation.
Nuts and seeds do not always have to be part of vegan cheeses.
Be a bit creative and develop new ideas and recipes based
on the basic recipes in this book.*

Ingredients

1 portion of basic cashew
cheese (see p. 30),
ripened for 1-2 days
150 g cooked millet,
cooled
1 tsp granulated garlic
1 tsp granulated onion
1½ tsp yeast flakes
½ tsp barley miso
50 ml soya drink
60 g coconut cooking fat,
liquid *or* soft
¾ tsp Himalayan salt

Servings

Makes about 500 g

- Put all the ingredients in a blender and mix until you have a creamy, homogenous mixture. If necessary, stop the machine several times throughout the process and scrape the mixture down towards the blade, then continue mixing.

- Line a small bowl with cling film, add the cheese mixture and chill in the refrigerator for several hours.

- Remove the cheese from the bowl, and sprinkle with dried herbs, if desired, before serving.

- The cheese can be kept in the refrigerator for about five days.

Cashew cheese fondue

Ingredients

100 g cashew nuts
150 ml white wine
100 ml rejuvelac
80 ml water
20 g corn oil *or another*
  neutral-tasting
  vegetable oil
2 tbsp yeast flakes
½ tsp Dijon mustard
½–¾ tsp barley miso *or*
  another light miso
1–1¼ tsp Himalayan salt
1 pinch turmeric
1 tbsp cornflour
20 ml water
1 clove garlic

Also:
High-powered blender
Cheese fondue pot

Servings

For 1-2 people

- Purée all the ingredients except the cornflour and the water in a high-powered blender to make a smooth mixture.

- Put the cashew mixture with the water in a saucepan and heat whilst stirring.

- Mix the cornflour with 20 ml water until smooth and stir into the almost boiling cashew mixture. Simmer briefly until the mixture has achieved a thick custard-like consistency.

- Rub the garlic around the fondue pot, pour the cashew and cheese mixture into the pot, and enjoy with a baguette or diced, boiled potatoes.

Tip — When thinned with a little water, this vegan cheese fondue is also suitable as a topping for a potato gratin.

Kuri squash mac-and-cheese

300 g macaroni

For the sauce:
1 small onion
1 tbsp coconut oil
200 g uchiki (red) kuri
   squash, diced
250 ml water
50 g cashew nuts
15 g coconut cooking fat
   or a neutral-tasting
   vegetable oil
1 small clove garlic
3-4 tsp yeast flakes
1–1½ tsp Himalayan salt
A little nutmeg
A little pepper

Servings

Makes 3 servings

• Cook the macaroni in salted water until al dente.

• Chop the onion and fry in the coconut oil until transparent. Add the diced squash and the water to the pan, put the lid on and cook for ten minutes until the squash is soft.

• Put the onion and squash mixture with the remaining ingredients in a robust blender and purée into a creamy sauce. If you do not have a robust blender, you can soak the cashew nuts in advance for four to six hours. In this case, use only 230 ml of water to cook the squash.

• Mix the cooked macaroni with the sauce and either enjoy immediately, or put in an oven-proof dish and bake for ten minutes in a preheated oven at 200°C, gas 6. Before baking, you can also sprinkle the dish with the grated cheese described on page 74.

Millet cheese cake
with date topping

Ingredients

For the almond base:
100 g almonds
2 tbsp concentrated
   agave syrup

For the millet mixture:
100 g cashew nuts
3 tbsp concentrated
   agave syrup
100 ml almond milk
5 drops of vanilla extract
150 g millet, cooked
   without salt
120 g coconut oil, liquid

Caramel topping:
40 g dates, pitted and
   soaked
20 ml water for soaking

Almond base:

- Finely grind the almonds in a standard blender. Add the concentrated agave syrup, mix again briefly until everything is combined.

- Divide the mixture between the little moulds and press down to form an even base.

Millet mixture:

- Mix the cashew nuts with the agave syrup, 50 ml almond milk and the vanilla extract in the blender. As soon as there is a fine, creamy mixture, add the cooked millet and the remaining 50 ml of the almond milk, and mix until the millet is completely chopped up. Then add the liquid coconut oil and mix until everything is well combined.

- Divide the mixture between the little moulds. Moisten your fingers in cold water and smooth down the mixture with your damp fingers.

- Chill in the refrigerator for several hours until the mixture is firm.

Also:

6 pecan *or* walnut halves

Silicone mould for little cakes, 7 cm diameter

Servings

Makes 6 mini tartlets

Date topping:

- Soak the dates for at least three hours in water. Then mix with about 20 ml of the water used for soaking until you have a smooth, viscous mixture.

- Spread the date topping on the cakes immediately before serving and decorate each one with half a pecan or walnut.

- Chill for several hours in the refrigerator before serving.

- The millet cheese cakes can be kept in the refrigerator for up to five days.

Pesto spread
from almond pulp

If you make a substantial quantity of almond drink, you will also have a lot of almond pulp left over. You can freeze it, and once you have a large quantity, defrost it and use it to make various spreads. Here is a quick example for using almond pulp with homemade wild garlic pesto. This recipe uses leftovers. It is more of a spread than a cheese.

Ingredients

200 g almond pulp
4 tbsp wild garlic pesto
   or another vegan
   pesto, as desired
1 tsp Himalayan salt
1–2 tbsp olive oil,
   optional

Servings

Makes about 300 g

- Mix all the ingredients in a blender until fine and creamy. If the mixture is too dry, add 1–2 tbsp of olive oil.

- Place cooking rings on greaseproof paper, fill with the mixture, press down firmly and chill in the refrigerator for several hours. As soon as it is firm enough, press the spread from the rings.

- The spread can be kept in the refrigerator for about three days.

Pizza cheese

This quickly made mixture based on almond paste is ideal to use as an alternative to cheese on pizzas. Although I also like to use all the cashew and almond cheese varieties on pizza bases too.

Ingredients

60 g almond paste, light

2 tbsp lemon juice

½ tsp yeast flakes

¼ tsp Himalayan salt

About 30 ml water

Servings

Around 11 cheese rounds of 6 cm each is enough for two small pizzas

- Mix the ingredients and stir in enough water to create a viscous mixture. The exact quantity of water depends on which almond paste is used. Use a blender to mix large quantities, or by hand for smaller quantities.

- To use the pizza cheese first bake your pizza bases at approximately 220°C, gas 7 without cheese.

- Five minutes before they are ready, take the pizza bases out of the oven and spread the almond paste mixture on top. Or if you want to create a round of cheese like mozzarella use 6 cm round cutters and spread the almond paste mixture in them using a spoon and slide onto the pizza base. Add any other toppings of your choice, such as cherry tomatoes.

- Put the pizzas back in the oven and bake for five minutes until the vegan cheese is a light golden brown in colour.

Cheese sauce for nachos

Ingredients

250 ml almond milk

1-1½ tbsp cornflour

30 ml neutral tasting vegetable oil

1 small clove garlic, crushed

6 tsp yeast flakes

1 tsp tomato purée

½ tsp barley miso

½ tsp mustard

½ tsp onion powder

½–¾ tsp Himalayan salt

Servings

Makes 280 ml

- Take a small quantity of the almond milk and use to stir into the cornflour to form a smooth paste.

- Put the other ingredients into a pan and bring to the boil.

- When the mixture is boiling, fold the cornflour, with a whisk, into the mixture and bring to the boil again briefly.

- Serve the cheese sauce warm, or cold, with nachos.

Grated cheese

This vegan alternative for Parmesan tastes delicious in all pasta dishes.

Ingredients

50 g almonds, blanched

50 g Macadamia nuts
(can be replaced by
other almonds)

1 tbsp sesame seeds

1 tbsp dry breadcrumbs

1 tbsp yeast flakes

½ tsp Himalayan salt

Servings

Makes 1 jar of grated
cheese

- Put all the ingredients in a blender and grind carefully until the nuts resemble grated Parmesan.

- This grated cheese will keep for several weeks in a jar with a lid.

Tofu with nigari

It is very easy to make tofu. You can make it with soya milk, either shop-bought or homemade.

Ingredients

8 g nigari flakes

2 litres soya milk, homemade

Also:

Tofu press

Cotton cloth

Servings

Makes about 190 g tofu

- Disolve the nigari flakes in a little warm water.

- I advise using the soya milk as soon as you have made it, as it has to be warmed up anyway.

- Heat the soya milk until almost boiling, carefully stir the nigari solution into the milk for a short time only. Stir in a circular motion once or twice so that the solid bits stay as coarse as possible. The whey usually separates immediately from the solid bits, sometimes it takes a little longer. If the whey does not separate immediately, leave it to stand for ten minutes. If the coagulation process has not started within ten minutes, heat the milk again and add a little more nigari solution.

- Put a sieve over a bowl and put the tofu press, lined with a cotton cloth, into the sieve. Carefully tip the tofu mixture into the cotton cloth until it is all in the press.

- As soon as the liquid has drained, take the press out of the sieve, fold the cloth over the tofu, put the press part of the mould in the sieve part and weigh the press down with as much weight as possible. Press the tofu for several hours or overnight.

- Then take the tofu out of the press and put it in a lidded container, cover the tofu with water and store in the refrigerator. The water must be changed every day.

- The tofu can be kept in the refrigerator for about three to four days.

Tip — Once the solid parts of the soya milk have separated from the whey, you can add various herbs (for example, basil, or *herbes de Provence*, or finely chopped olives) to the milk to give you new varieties of tofu. Nigari is not easy to obtain. The simplest way is to order it over the internet.

Tofu with lemon juice

Tofu with lemon juice can be used as a vegan alternative to Indian paneer dishes. It is somewhat softer than tofu with nigari.

Ingredients

2 litres soya milk, homemade

7-8 tbsp lemon juice

Also:
Tofu press
Cotton cloth

Servings

Makes about 190 g tofu

• Pour the homemade soya milk into a pan, add 7–8 tbsp of lemon juice, stir and heat almost to boiling point.

• Remove the soya milk from the hob and wait until the whey separates from the solids. This usually happens immediately. In exceptional cases, it takes up to ten minutes. If the whey has not separated from the solids after the waiting time, you can help it along by reheating and adding more lemon juice. As soon as the whey has separated, drain it off the mixture.

• Either put the mixture into the tofu press, lined with a cloth and place in a sieve or if you don't have a tofu press place a muslin cloth in the sieve and gradually pour the tofu mixture into the sieve. If you are using a tofu press and there is not enough space in the press for anymore tofu mixture (depending on the size of the mould), you should allow it to drain for a few minutes each time.

• Fold the cotton cloth over the tofu, weight down the tofu and put everything in a cool place overnight.

- Then put the tofu in a lidded container, cover the tofu with water and store in the refrigerator. The water must be changed every day.

- The tofu can be kept in the refrigerator for about three to four days.

Tip — If like me, you cannot tolerate shop-bought tofu, try one of these two homemade versions. I can tolerate these much better.

Tip — Instead of lemon juice, you can also use cider vinegar.

Silken tofu

*I first encountered silken tofu many years ago in Beijing.
It was served marinated with lots of spring onions or chives,
soy sauce and sesame oil. Shop-bought silken tofu is made
a little differently to the version that can be made at home.
The result is, however, very similar.*

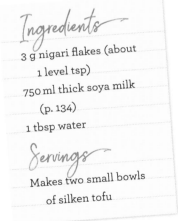

Ingredients

3 g nigari flakes (about
1 level tsp)

750 ml thick soya milk
(p. 134)

1 tbsp water

Servings

Makes two small bowls
of silken tofu

- Dissolve the nigari flakes in 1 tablespoon of lukewarm water and carefully stir into the cooled thick soya milk. Stir round just once or twice slowly until everything is well mixed. Do not stir too much! The milk must be cool otherwise the cheese will separate from the whey as soon as the nigari solution is stirred into it.

- Fill two little bowls with the mixture and steam for ten minutes in a steamer or a wok with a bamboo basket. Leave to cool.

- The silken tofu can be kept in the refrigerator for about three to four days.

Tip — Nigari is not easy to obtain. The simplest way is to order it over the internet.

Shan
or chickpea tofu

*Shan is an ideal alternative for anyone allergic to soya.
It can be used in Indian paneer dishes or as an alternative
to mozzarella in Italian caprese salad. Chickpea tofu is
really quick and simple to make yourself.*

Ingredients

200 g chickpea flour

800 ml water

2 tsp Himalayan salt

½ tsp turmeric, ground

Also:

Mould, about 15 cm x 15
cm and 6 cm high

A little oil to grease
the dish

Servings

Makes about 900 g

- Mix the chickpea flour with the water, salt and turmeric until smooth. This can be done quickly with a stick blender.

- Put the mixture in a large saucepan and bring to the boil whilst stirring. Cook the mixture on a low heat until transparent. Continue to stir, so that it does not burn. The mixture will be ready in four to five minutes.

- In the meantime, grease a small baking dish or the lower half of a storage container with oil and pour the mixture in. Smooth it down and and chill overnight.

- Turn the mixture out the next day and cut into cubes with a large knife.

- Shan tofu can be baked, or fried in oil, or marinated cold and eaten with a salad.

Tip — Sear shan tofu on both sides in coconut oil and enjoy with a leaf salad. If using as mozzarella with tomatoes, add a few dried herbs, such as basil or oregano, to the mixture.

Tip — Chickpea flour is available in well-stocked healthfood or Asian shops.

Cream, yoghurt and Co.

Cream, yoghurt and Co. based on nuts
and soya can also be made simply.
For those allergic to soya, there are
also soya-free versions.

Cashew nut crème fraîche

This is my favourite version of crème fraîche.

Ingredients

200 g cashew nuts
50-70 ml water
3-4 tbsp lemon juice
¼ tsp Himalayan salt

Servings

Makes about 300-350 ml

- Soak the cashew nuts in water overnight.

- The next day pour off the water, rinse and drain. Put them in a blender or food processor with the fresh water, lemon juice and salt. Mix until reduced to small pieces.

- Depending on how firm you want the crème fraîche to be, adjust the quantity of water.

Tip — I use a high-powered blender to make crème fraîche. Soaked cashew nuts can also be chopped up finely using a stick blender's mixing jug.

Fermented almond crème fraîche

Crème fraîche made with rejuvelac and almonds is more acidic than the sweeter cashew version.

Ingredients

150 g blanched almonds
150 ml rejuvelac
100 ml water

Servings

Makes about 270 ml

- Put all the ingredients in a high-powered blender and blend until you have a fine, creamy mixture. Pour the mixture into a jar. Do not fill more than three-quarters full as the crème fraîche will increase in volume during the fermentation process.

- Put a cheesecloth on the jar, fix with a rubber band and leave to ferment in a warm place. Avoid direct sunlight.

- Depending on your room temperature, the fermentation process will take approximately 16 hours in summer, and longer in winter. Using a clean spoon, taste from time to time to see if it has reached the required acidity.

- Put the crème fraîche in the refrigerator and chill for a few hours. The mixture will become a little thicker in the refrigerator. Stir the crème fraîche through before using. It will reduce slightly in volume as a result.

- This fermented crème fraîche can be kept in the refrigerator for about three days.

Tip — You will need a powerful blender for this recipe.

Sour cream
made from cashew nuts

*My preferred versions of cream are those
based on cashews.*

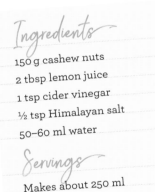

Ingredients

150 g cashew nuts
2 tbsp lemon juice
1 tsp cider vinegar
½ tsp Himalayan salt
50–60 ml water

Servings

Makes about 250 ml

- Soak the cashew nuts overnight.

- The next day, rinse the nuts and mix with the other ingredients using a stick blender or food processor until you have a homogenous mixture.

- This sour cream can be kept in the refrigerator for about three days.

Sour cream
made from soya yoghurt

This sour cream is made without cashew nuts and consists mainly of soya yoghurt.

Ingredients

500 ml soya yoghurt,
homemade *or*
shop-bought

Also:
Muslin cloth

Servings

Makes about 280 g,
depending on the
yoghurt and how
long it takes to drain

- Place the muslin cloth in a sieve. Put the sieve in a bowl or saucepan that is deeper than the sieve so that its base does not touch the bottom.

- Put the yoghurt in the muslin cloth and put in the refrigerator. Once the yoghurt has drained for 12-20 hours, you can use it as a vegan alternative to sour cream. The exact draining time depends very much on the yoghurt used as they differ from manufacturer to manufacturer.

- This sour cream can be kept in the refrigerator for about three to four days.

Cashew mascarpone

This cashew nut and almond milk mascarpone can be made in a sweet version as well.

Ingredients

400 g cashew nuts

150 ml almond milk

For the sweet version:
3–4 tbsp raw cane sugar
and optional ¼–½ tsp
vanilla powder

For the tiramisu cream:
Additional 2 tbsp brandy

Servings

Makes about 720 ml

- Soak the cashew nuts in water overnight.

- The next day, rinse them, drain and mix with the almond milk in a powerful blender. It works with a stick blender too, but the mixture will not be as fine. In this case, prepare the cream in two portions. Depending on the blender's power, you may need a little more almond milk to obtain a smooth mixture.

- If the cashew mascarpone is going to be used for tiramisu, you can add all the ingredients at the mixing stage and mix together.

- The mascarpone can be kept in the refrigerator for two to three days.

Tip — As the exact quantity of liquid depends greatly on the soaking time and the type of blender used, add just a little almond milk to the blender initially and then continue to add as necessary to create a creamy mixture.

Tiramisu

Ingredients

1 portion of the
    sweet version of
    mascarpone on
    page 94, made with
    sugar and brandy.

For the sponge:
160 g sugar
1 tbsp vanilla sugar
250 ml soya *or* almond
    milk
135 ml corn oil
2 tbsp cider vinegar
250 g wheat flour
5 tsp cream of tartar
2 pinches turmeric,
    ground

Sponge:

- Preheat the oven to 180°C, gas 4.

- Line a baking sheet with greaseproof paper.

- Mix the sugar with the vanilla sugar, soya milk, oil and the vinegar.

- Stir in the wheat flour, cream of tartar and turmeric into the mixture until you have got rid of all the lumps. The batter should be stirred quickly and only for as long as absolutely necessary.

- Pour the mixture onto the greaseproof paper and spread evenly over the baking sheet, but do not cover the baking sheet entirely.

- Place the baking sheet into the pre-heated oven and bake for 18–23 minutes until the edge is slightly light brown and nothing sticks to a skewer when you test it. The precise baking time depends on your oven and the thickness of the batter.

- Remove the sponge from the oven and allow to cool.

Tiramisu:

- Place a fresh sheet of greaseproof paper on the cooled sponge, turn the sponge over and carefully remove the sheet that was in the oven. Depending on the size of the

Also:

1–1½ large cups of
espresso

Cocoa powder,
unsweetened

Round biscuit cutters,
approx 5.5 cm
diameter, depending
on diameter of jar

Servings

Makes 9 small glass jars

glass jars to be used to serve the dessert, cut the sponge to the right size using a biscuit cutter and place the sponge circles aside.

• Pour the coffee into a deep bowl.

• Dip each sponge circle into the coffee for as short a time as possible and then put in a glass jar until each has a sponge base. Spread some cream on the sponge. Dip a second sponge circle in the coffee and place on top of the layer of cream and finish off by adding a second layer of cream.

• Leave the tiramisu to stand for several hours or overnight in the refrigerator. Before serving, sift the cocoa over the top of the tiramisu.

• The tiramisu will keep for about four days in the refrigerator.

Tip — If you bake the sponge for other purposes, use 10 g less sugar. It has to be a little sweeter for tiramisu.

Quark substitute
made from soya yoghurt

*Soya yoghurt is suitable as a base for
a straightforward alternative to quark.*

Ingredients

500 ml soya yoghurt,
homemade *or*
shop-bought

Also:
Muslin cloth

Servings

Makes about 250 g,
depending on how
long it takes to drain

- Put the muslin in a sieve above a bowl or saucepan that is deeper than the sieve so that its base does not touch the bottom.

- Put the yoghurt in the muslin cloth and put the sieve and container in the refrigerator. Allow the yoghurt to drain for 48–72 hours. The exact draining time depends very much on the yoghurt used as they differ from manufacturer to manufacturer.

- After the draining stage, it can be kept in the refrigerator for about three to four days.

Cashew ricotta

*As a great fan of Italian cuisine, it goes without saying that
I would have to include a vegan version of ricotta in this book.
I particularly like cashew ricotta on fresh bread with
artichokes in oil on top.*

Ingredients

150 g cashew nuts
30 ml kombucha
1 tsp Himalayan salt

Servings

Makes about 235 g

- Soak the cashew nuts overnight.

- The next day, pour off the water, rinse and drain. Mix the cashew nuts with the kombucha and salt using a stick blender until smooth.

- Put the mixture in a glass or ceramic bowl, cover with a plate and allow to ferment for one to one-and-a-half days at room temperature. The taste will be stronger depending on the external temperature and the ripening time. Once the ricotta has reached the required intensity, it should be stored in the refrigerator until used.

- The ricotta can be kept in the refrigerator for about four to five days.

Cashew cream

There are two ways of making cashew cream. Version 1 is more suitable for powerful blenders, whereas version 2 works well with a less powerful machine.

Ingredients

80 g cashew nuts

160 ml water

Servings

Makes about 300 ml

Version 1:

- Grind the cashew nuts finely in a dry blender.
- Then add the water and mix on the highest setting for about a minute.

Version 2:

- Soak the cashew nuts overnight.
- The next day, mix the cashews with fresh water until the mixture is fine enough..

Tip — If you are in a hurry, you can mix ready-made cashew paste with a little water.

Tip — Cashew cream is perfect to make nice ice cream and cream of vegetable soups even creamier. It can also be used effectively in vegan ice cream.

Whippable coconut cream

Chill the coconut milk overnight – or preferably for 24 hours.
Also chill a metal bowl and the mixer attachments for an hour.
Make sure you buy pure coconut milk, without stabilisers.
Stabilisers will make it difficult for the solids and liquids to
separate. The whippable coconut cream is perfect for cold desserts
and cake. It will liquefy again in a warm atmosphere.

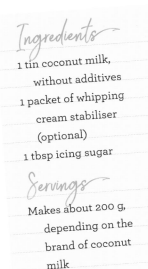

Ingredients

1 tin coconut milk,
without additives
1 packet of whipping
cream stabiliser
(optional)
1 tbsp icing sugar

Servings

Makes about 200 g,
depending on the
brand of coconut
milk

- Take the coconut milk out of the refrigerator, open, and using a spoon, carefully remove the solid coconut milk.

- Beat the solid mass until stiff for one to two minutes with a stick blender. It will depend on the brand as to how firm the coconut cream becomes. If it does not become firm enough, you can mix more whipping cream stabiliser in at the end. Stir in the icing sugar as required right at the end.

- If you chill the cream after beating, for about an hour, it will become even firmer.

Tip — The liquid part still in the tin is not required and can be used for smoothies or shakes.

Tip — Normal coconut milk is also suitable as a cream substitute for making vegan ice cream.

Soya yoghurt
with agar agar

Soya yoghurt has a life of its own. In order to obtain the exact recipe, you have to have the same conditions. The soya milk manufacturer, the starter brand, and the yoghurt machine play an important role. If you want to make soya yoghurt, you will need a little patience to develop the perfect recipe.

Ingredients

½–1 tsp agar agar powder
500 ml soya milk,
  homemade *or*
  shop-bought
1 tsp or 2 g vegan yoghurt
  starter (*or* depending
  on the manufacturer,
  the quantity for 500 ml
  of yoghurt)

Also:
Yoghurt maker

Servings

Makes 500 ml

• Put the agar agar powder in a saucepan with 200 ml soya milk and whisk well by hand. Bring to the boil and simmer on a low heat for two minutes, stirring constantly.

• Then stir in the remaining soya milk and let it all cool down.

• When the liquid is lukewarm, stir in the yoghurt starter. Pour the yoghurt base into small glasses and put them in the yoghurt maker without lids. Close the lid of the yoghurt maker, turn it on and set the time switch to eight hours. Do not move or shake the yoghurt maker during this period.

• When the yoghurt is ready, chill it for several hours. If the yoghurt is too thin, the fermentation time can be increased by up to two hours, if necessary.

• The yoghurt can be kept in the refrigerator for about three to four days.

Slightly sweetened soya yoghurt

In this recipe, the sugar has the effect of making the yoghurt medium firm without adding any agar agar powder. The exact consistency depends on the brand of soya drink and the yoghurt starter used.

Ingredients

1 tsp raw cane sugar

500 ml soya milk, homemade *or* shop-bought

1 tsp or 2 g vegan yoghurt starter (*or* depending on the manufacturer, the quantity for ½ litre of yoghurt)

Servings

Makes 500 ml

• Heat up the soya milk. Stir in the sugar and leave to cool down.

• As soon as the soya milk is lukewarm, the yoghurt starter can be stirred in with a whisk. Pour the yoghurt base into small glasses and put them in the yoghurt maker without lids. Close the lid of the yoghurt maker, turn it on and set the time switch to ten hours. Do not move or shake the yoghurt maker during this period.

• When the yoghurt is ready, chill it for several hours.

• The yoghurt can be kept in the refrigerator for about three to four days.

Coconut and almond yoghurt

A delicious vegan yoghurt can be made based on coconut and almond milks. Use purchased coconut milk as the consistency is different to homemade.

Ingredients

¾–1 level tsp agar agar powder

300 ml almond milk

200 ml coconut milk

1 tsp (2 g) vegan yoghurt starter (*or depending on the manufacturer, the quantity for 500 ml of yoghurt*)

Servings

Makes about 500 ml

- Stir the agar agar into 100 ml of almond milk, bring to the boil and simmer for two to three minutes while stirring.

- Stir the remaining almond milk and coconut milk into the agar agar mixture and leave the yoghurt base to cool for a short time.

- As soon as the mixture is lukewarm, the yoghurt starter can be stirred with a balloon whisk. Pour the yoghurt base into small glasses and put them in the yoghurt maker without lids. Close the lid of the yoghurt maker, turn it on and set the time switch to ten hours. Do not move or shake the yoghurt maker during this period. Then remove the glasses from the yoghurt maker and put the lids on.

- When the yoghurt is ready, chill it for several hours. It will become firmer in the refrigerator.

- The yoghurt can be kept in the refrigerator for two to three days.

Raw vegan
cashew yoghurt

This raw vegan cashew yoghurt is a wonderful accompaniment to crunchy granola muesli with fruit. The yoghurt turns sour and I think it tastes best on its second day. Together with the coconut-and-almond yoghurt, this yoghurt is my favourite vegan yoghurt.

Ingredients

200 g cashew nuts

330 ml water

1 level tsp vegan yoghurt starter

Servings

Makes about 500 ml

- Soak the cashew nuts overnight.

- The next day, rinse the nuts and mix with the fresh yoghurt and yoghurt starter in a blender.

- Pour the liquid into glasses, but do not fill to the top, as the mixture gains volume during the fermentation process. Put the glasses in a cotton cloth or tea-towel and close with a rubber band and leave to ferment in a warm place for 12-24 hours, depending on the room temperature. Keep the yoghurt out of draughts and direct sunlight during this time. Test the yoghurt carefully with a clean spoon to see if it tastes right for you. The longer it ferments, the stronger and more acidic it will taste.

- Then put the lids on the glasses and put them in the refrigerator for several hours. Stir through before serving. If the yoghurt is too firm, stir a little water into it until it is the right consistency.

- The yoghurt can be kept in the refrigerator for two to three days.

Tip — The firmness of the yoghurt will depend on various factors (fermentation, room temperature, soaking time, etc.).

Cashew yoghurt
with rejuvelac
(and almond yoghurt alternative)

*Yoghurt does not have to be made with shop-bought cultures.
You can ferment a nut mixture with homemade rejuvelac. Rejuvelac
yoghurts taste a little more acidic than those made with a yoghurt starter.
The cashew version is finer, whereas the almond version has a stronger
taste and is firmer. Personally, I prefer the cashew version.*

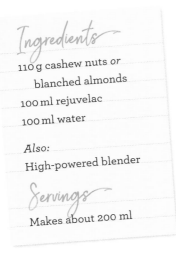

Ingredients

110 g cashew nuts *or*
    blanched almonds
100 ml rejuvelac
100 ml water

Also:
High-powered blender

Servings

Makes about 200 ml

• Put all the ingredients in a high-powered blender and blend until you have a fine, creamy mixture.

• Pour the mixture into a jar. Do not fill more than three-quarters full as the yoghurt will increase in volume during the fermentation process. Put a cheesecloth on the jar, fix with a rubber band and leave to ferment in a warm place. Do not stand the yoghurt in direct sunlight.

• The fermentation process will take between 10 and 15 hours, depending on the room temperature and the desired taste. The longer it ferments, the stronger it will taste. Using a clean spoon carefullly test to see if it has reached the required acidity and firmness.

• The almond version of the finished yoghurt is really thick and can be adjusted to the required consistency by adding around 20–30 ml water and stirring.

• Put the yoghurt in the refrigerator and enjoy chilled. The yoghurt will be firmer after chilling.

• The yoghurt can be kept in the refrigerator for about three to four days.

Tip— You will need a powerful blender for this recipe.

Olive oil butter

Homemade vegan butter has the advantage of not using any palm oil. This recipe uses olive oil as a base.

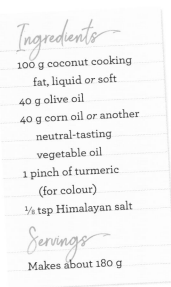

Ingredients

100 g coconut cooking
    fat, liquid *or* soft

40 g olive oil

40 g corn oil *or* another
    neutral-tasting
    vegetable oil

1 pinch of turmeric
    (for colour)

1/8 tsp Himalayan salt

Servings

Makes about 180 g

- Mix all the ingredients using a stick blender until the salt has dissolved.

- Then put the mixture in small silicon muffin trays and chill in the refrigerator for several hours.

- The olive oil butter can then be kept in the refrigerator or stored in the freezer until needed. It will keep in the refrigerator for about five days.

Tip — As olive oil butter is very soft and melts easily, we prefer to use it in winter. Soya butter is better on toast, warm bread or pastries.

Soya butter

As homemade vegan butters, such as this soya butter, do not keep for very long, I recommend you put it in small containers and freeze it. Defrost small portions as required.

Ingredients

120 g soya milk, homemade *or* shop-bought
200 g coconut cooking fat, liquid *or* soft
2 tsp sunflower lecithin
2 pinches of turmeric (for colour)
1 pinch Himalayan salt

Servings

Makes about 320 g

- Put all the ingredients in a blender and mix until the salt has dissolved and the mixture is well emulsified.

- Pour the mixture into small silicon or flexible plastic moulds and chill in the refrigerator for several hours until the butter is hard.

- The soya butter can be kept in the refrigerator for about five days.

Tip — This recipe also works with almond milk as well as soya milk. However, you will then need to use 2½–3 tsp of sunflower lecithin so that the mixture emulsifies. Although I usually prefer products without soya, I think the soya version of this butter tastes better.

Millet butter

This millet butter is a lower fat mixture of butter substitute and spread.

Ingredients

50 g cashew nuts, soaked
100 g cooked millet, cooled
1 tbsp lemon juice
½ tsp Himalayan salt
50 g coconut cooking fat, liquid *or* soft
2 pinches of turmeric (for colour)
30–40 ml water

Servings

Makes about 250 g

- Soak the cashew nuts overnight. Cook the millet, then leave to cool.

- Put all the ingredients in a blender and mix until the cashews and millet are chopped into small pieces. If necessary, add some more water. Depending on your blender, stop it several times throughout the process and scrape the mixture towards the blade.

- The butter can be kept in the refrigerator for about five days. Remove it from the refrigerator a few minutes before using otherwise it will be very hard. This millet butter can be frozen in small portions and defrosted as required.

Tips for cooking millet—

- 150 g millet and 150 ml water produce around 270 g cooked millet.
- Wash the millet well, first with hot, then with cold water. Then bring to the boil with the water in a small saucepan covered with a lid. The water should cover the millet by approx. 1 cm.
- As soon as the millet boils, turn the heat down to its lowest setting and simmer covered for 20 minutes. Remove from the hob and steep for ten minutes.

Vegan drinks

These homemade vegan milk substitutes leave nothing to be desired when making coffee, shakes, desserts or ice cream.

Almond milk

*This is my absolute favourite drink and I love it in coffee.
It is also my first choice for making shakes and desserts.
The almond pulp left over from making drinks can be
frozen and then defrosted when needed to make into
spreads for sandwiches.*

Ingredients

100 g almonds
1 litre water
Nut milk bag *or* cotton
cloth

Also:
High-powered blender

Servings

Makes 1 litre

- Soak the almonds overnight.

- The next day, rinse them and blitz with a litre of water in a high-powered blender for about a minute. If you would like the drink to be sweet, add in two or three stoned dates before blitzing.

- Strain the liquid through the nut milk bag or muslin, pour into a bottle and store in the refrigerator. Shake well before use.

- This almond milk can be kept in the refrigerator for two to three days. If it is a particularly hot summer, it may only keep until the next day.

Quick nut drink

If you are in a hurry, or you do not own a powerful blender, then this is the perfect recipe. You can make vegan nut drinks quickly and easily with a jar of nut paste. The recipe makes a litre of liquid. It makes sense to make only the required quantity so that it is fresh.

Ingredients

4 tbsp (100 g) nut paste,
as desired

1 litre water

Servings

Makes 1 litre

- Mix the nut paste with a little water using a blender or a stick blender. Small smoothie mixers can also be used.

- When everything is well mixed, add the remaining water and mix again briefly, then pour the liquid through a fine sieve.

- It will keep in the refrigerator for about a day.

Hemp milk

Like hemp seeds themselves, hemp drink has a strong distinctive taste. This drink with its high fat content is best suited to smooth, sweet milkshakes. I like to use it mixed in equal parts with almond milk, and a 2 cm vanilla pod for a creamy Matcha shake.

Ingredients

100 g hemp seeds, hulled

1 litre water

Servings

Makes 1 litre

- Put the hemp seeds into a blender with the water and mix until all the seeds have been chopped up.

- Pour the liquid through a nut milk bag, and squeeze out the seed residue well. There will be almost no residue left in the bag. Pour the liquid into a bottle and store in the refrigerator. Shake well before use.

- Hemp milk keeps in the refrigerator for about a day.

Cashew milk

Cashew nuts are also very good for making drinks, particularly shakes, if you add fresh fruit such as strawberries or bananas.

Ingredients

80 g cashew nuts

1 litre water

Servings

Makes 1 litre

- Soak the cashew nuts overnight.

- The next morning, rinse them and blitz with a litre of water in a high-powered blender for about a minute.

- Pour the liquid into a muslin cloth or a nut milk bag. Allow to drain, and squeeze out the cashew mixture.

- Pour the liquid into a bottle and store in the refrigerator. Shake the milk well before use.

- This cashew milk can be kept in the refrigerator for two to three days.

Buckwheat milk

Buckwheat milk can be made either with buckwheat soaked overnight or, as in this recipe, with germinated buckwheat. It has a strong flavour and is therefore best suited to making shakes.

Ingredients

80 g buckwheat

1 litre water

Also:
High-powered blender

Servings

Makes 1 litre

- Soak the buckwheat in water overnight. The next day, drain, rinse well in fresh water and put in a jar. Fasten a cotton cloth or kitchen paper round the top of the jar with a rubber band. Rinse the buckwheat thoroughly every morning and evening until you can see it sprouting.

- Mix the buckwheat sprouts with a litre of cold water in a high-powered blender for about a minute.

- Strain through a muslin cloth or nut milk bag, pour into bottles and store in the refrigerator. Shake the milk well before use.

- It will keep for one to two days in the refrigerator.

Soya milk (machine method)

*If you wish to make soya milk on a regular basis,
I recommend investing in a soya milk machine. Using one
means making soya milk is considerably faster and simpler.
In contrast to commercial versions, homemade soya milk is light
in colour and does not taste strongly of soya.*

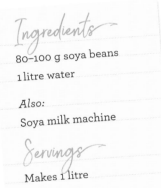

Ingredients

80–100 g soya beans

1 litre water

Also:
Soya milk machine

Servings

Makes 1 litre

• Soak the soya beans in water overnight. The next morning, rinse the beans and put them in the soya milk machine's sieve. Secure the sieve (depending on the machine) and start the soya milk programme.

• When ready, strain the soya milk through a muslin cloth or nut milk bag, cool, and store in the refrigerator. Shake well before use.

• Wash up all the utensils used immediately as soya milk sets and makes washing up later more difficult.

• The milk can be kept in the refrigerator for about three to four days..

Soya milk (saucepan method)

Here is a version made in a saucepan you can use to try out homemade soya milk as a drink or for using in silken tofu. You will need a high-powered blender for this recipe.

Ingredients

100–200 g soya beans

1 litre water

Also:

High-powered blender

Servings

Makes almost 1 litre

- Soak the soya beans in water overnight.

- The next morning, rinse the soya beans and blend them in a high-powered blender into a homogenous mixture with 500 ml water.

- In a large saucepan (the milk foams a lot) bring 500 ml water to the boil, add the soya mixture and bring to the boil again, stirring continuously. As soon as it boils, turn the heat down to medium and cook the milk for ten minutes, stirring continously. At the beginning, the milk will set (particularly if there is a large quantity of soya beans). You will have to stir vigorously and thoroughly. Towards the end of the cooking time, the milk will set less firmly, but it must be stirred well, right until it is ready.

- Strain the soya mixture through a nut milk bag or muslin. Press the cloth out thoroughly and let the milk cool before putting it in the refrigerator. Shake the milk well before use.

- The milk can be used immediately to make tofu. It must be cooled to make silken tofu, and be at least lukewarm for soya yoghurt.

- The milk can be kept in the refrigerator for about three to four days.

Tip — If making silken tofu, you will need thicker milk, so use 200 g soya beans.

Oat milk

When making oat milk, chilled mixing is crucial. Otherwise you will quickly produce gruel that cannot be strained. The milk is particularly good for mueslis, porridge and shakes.

Ingredients

80 g oats

5 dates

5 ice cubes

1 litre cold water

Servings

Makes 1 litre

- Put the oats, stoned dates, ice cubes and the cold water in a blender and blitz for one minute. The ice cubes are important as warm oat milk will quickly turn into gruel.

- Strain the mixture through a muslin cloth or nut milk bag, pour into bottles and store in the refrigerator. Shake well before use.

- Oat milk will keep for about two days in the refrigerator.

Coconut milk

This exotic coconut drink is perfect for summery, southern-style shakes. It is also delicious mixed in a powerful blender with fresh turmeric and small pieces of frozen banana.

Ingredients

150 g coconut flakes, dried

1 litre water

Also:
High-powered blender

Servings

Makes 1 litre

- Mix the coconut flakes with the water for about a minute in a high-powered blender until everything is chopped up.

- Then strain the milk through a muslin cloth or nut milk bag, pour into a bottle and store in the refrigerator. Shake well before use.

- This coconut milk keeps in the refrigerator for a day.

Fermented cashew buttermilk

Cashew buttermilk is made by fermenting cashew milk with rejuvelac.

Ingredients

250 ml water
110 g cashew nuts
¼ tsp salt
170 ml rejuvelac

Servings

Makes about 500 ml

- Mix the water and the cashew nuts with the salt in a powerful blender.

- Stir the rejuvelac into the liquid. Pour the liquid into a jar or a bottle with a wide neck and close the opening with a muslin cloth secured with a rubber band.

- In the summer the buttermilk will ferment in about 24 hours. It will take longer when the temperature is cooler. The longer it ferments, the stronger the taste will be.

- This cashew buttermilk can be kept in the refrigerator for two to three days. Stir carefully before using.

About the author

As a young girl, Yvonne Hölzl-Singh discovered her love of cooking and was responsible for producing ice creams, desserts and cakes. For the past four years, she has followed a vegan lifestyle and shares her best recipes and her own creations on her food blog to inspire everyone to cook.

Acknowledgements

My sincere thanks to you who have flicked through this book, read through it, or cooked your way through it.
To you, who in buying this book, have placed a lot of trust in me! A heartfelt thank you is due to my family and my friends for understanding that I had to go into 'hiding' for a long time while writing the book. Another heartfelt thank you is extended to my husband who has patiently endured the chaos caused by writing a cookbook for a second time. And particular thanks to Hannes for proof-reading.
But I would also like to thank all my cheese tasters, too. And sincere thanks are also extended to the wonderful team who have made this book possible. I should particularly like to mention Antje Munk and Lisa Seibel who have guided me gently through the creative process of producing a book. Many thanks!

I thank you all from my heart! Danke, Grazie & Merci!

Yvonne Hölzl-Singh

Index

GRUB STREET
#Vegan

Vegan Bible
Marie Laforêt
978-1-910690-07-9

Vegan BBQ
Nadine Horn & Jörg Mayer
978-1-910690-52-9

Raw Cakes
Caroline Fibaek
978-1-909808-05-8

**Vegan Recipes from
the Middle East**
Parvin Razavi
978-1-910690-37-6

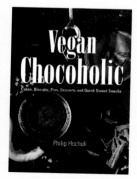

Vegan Chocoholic
*Cakes, Biscuits, Pies, Desserts
and Quick Sweet Snacks*
Philip Hochuli
978-1-910690-32-1